ISBN 978 1 941012 08 6

Library of Congress Control Number: 2014955900

Published by Emblem Media, LLC
505 Periwinkle, Fort Myers, FL 33908

Find us at: **www.emblemmediallc.com**

· GRANDPA'S ·
TIMEOUT

To my grandkids,
THE JOY OF AN OLD SOUL.

There was a lot of excitement in the Jones' home.

GRANDPA & GRANDMA WERE COMING!

David, Johnny and Michael could hardly contain themselves. Their grandparents always brought bags full of fun surprises whenever they came for a visit.

The boys had barely finished a late breakfast when they heard a car pull up in the driveway. They ran to the window. "It's Grandpa and Grandma!" The jumping and giggling started as soon as Grandpa and Grandma walked in the door. "Alright boys, settle down. Give them some room," Mommy ordered as she took their coats.

"Where should I put this?" Grandpa said, pointing at his big brown suitcase. "What's in there?" asked David, the oldest brother. "Oh…just some little surprises, but I'll show them to you later," Grandpa said with a wink.

After lunch, Mommy and Grandma decided to go and do a little shopping, leaving Grandpa to watch the boys.

Mommy wrote down everything Grandpa would need to know and told the boys to make sure they listened to him. It was very important for them to be on good behavior. The boys said they would listen to Grandpa, then they waved goodbye as Mommy and Grandma left.

Mommy forgot to tell Grandpa that *HE* also needed to be on good behavior.

Grandpa's List

1. No playing on furniture
2. No sweets before dinner
3. Let Spot out when he barks
4. No climbing big tree
5. Fill Spot's water bowl
6. Close fridge door after snack
7. Misbehavior = Timeout
8.

Michael

As soon as the ladies were out of sight Grandpa said, "Now let's have some fun! Let's play *The Jump Game*." "What's *The Jump Game*?" said Michael, the youngest. He had never played *The Jump Game* with Grandpa before. "*The Jump Game* is when we jump as high as we can all over the house," yelled Johnny, the middle boy.

The boys knew that Mommy didn't let them jump on the furniture, but since Grandpa said they could, it must be OK. So they all started jumping around the house. "See who can jump the highest!" laughed Grandpa. They were jumping off of their beds, the couches and even the table. Higher and higher they jumped. They were having so much fun they lost track of time.

Suddenly, Mommy and Grandma walked in
and completely surprised Grandpa and the boys.
Mommy dropped her bags and yelled,

"STOP!!!"

"YOU KNOW YOU ARE NOT
SUPPOSED TO JUMP ON
THE FURNITURE."

The boys all dropped to the floor.

Johnny shrugged and said, "But Grandpa said we could." "That may be true," said Mommy, "but Mommy and Daddy have told you not to do that, and you listen to us." She told the boys that they had to go to their timeout corners because they disobeyed.

Grandpa was embarrassed so he put his head down and said, "I'm sorry! It's my fault. I will also have a timeout, too." Grandma just shook her head and took her bags into the guestroom while Mommy went into the kitchen to cool down for a minute.

After timeout was over, the boys asked Grandpa if they
could see inside his special suitcase. Grandpa said, "Sure,
come take a look!" He opened his suitcase and the boys'
eyes widened. What a surprise! It was filled with candy!
"Let's have a candy-eating party," Grandpa said as he started
piling it in their hands. The boys looked at each other knowing
they needed to ask Mommy before eating the candy, but
since Grandpa gave it to them they thought it might be OK.

So, when Mommy walked into the room and saw everyone sitting on the floor with their mouths stuffed with candy and surrounded by empty candy wrappers, she was not happy. "What in the world are you doing?" she asked with her hands on her hips. "I gave the boys candy to make them happy," said Grandpa. "You may be making them happy," Mommy said, "but you are also making them sick." Then she looked to the boys and said, "Go wash your hands and mouths and then come back." They lowered their heads and walked out.

When they came back in the room, Michael looked up sheepishly and asked, "Are we getting another timeout?" "No timeout this time," said Mommy. "I'm giving you a job. Here is a garbage bag. You need to put all of the candy in it and then take it out to the trash can."

It was not a fun job for the boys to fill the bag with all of the candy and drag it out to the garbage can.

Dinner was very quiet that evening. The boys weren't
hungry because they had eaten so much candy. They were
just picking at their plates. Mommy had made a nice dessert,
but the boys weren't allowed to have any since they had
so much sugar earlier and didn't eat their dinner. Grandpa
said he wouldn't have dessert either, since it was his fault
that the boys couldn't have any.

There were no other problems the rest of the evening.
Everyone seemed relieved to go to bed and bring the day
to a peaceful end.

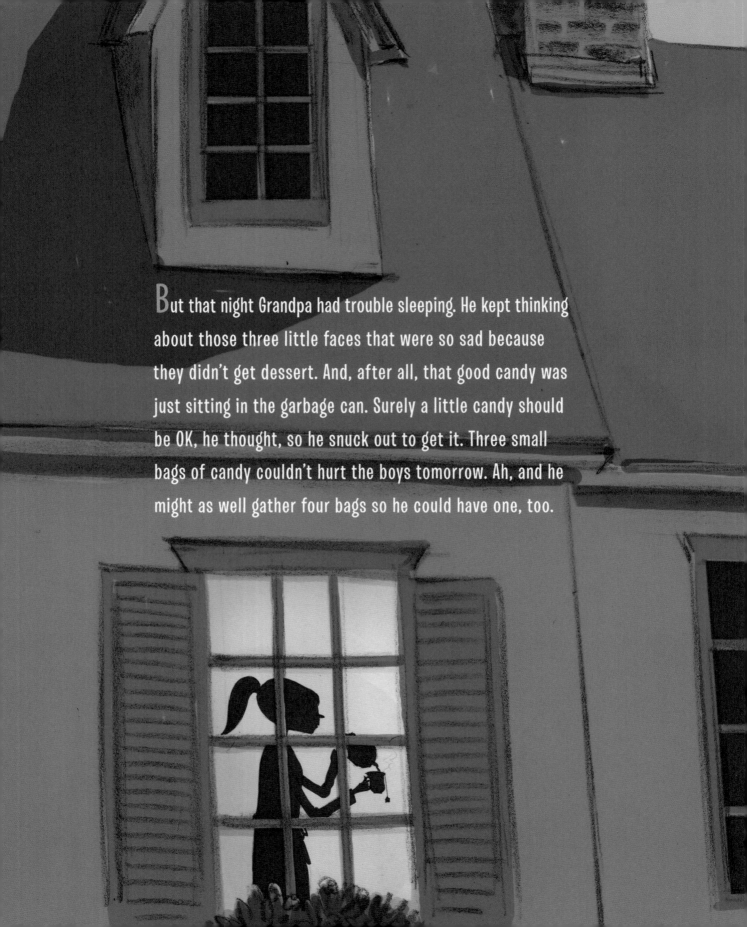

But that night Grandpa had trouble sleeping. He kept thinking about those three little faces that were so sad because they didn't get dessert. And, after all, that good candy was just sitting in the garbage can. Surely a little candy should be OK, he thought, so he snuck out to get it. Three small bags of candy couldn't hurt the boys tomorrow. Ah, and he might as well gather four bags so he could have one, too.

As he tried to sneak quietly back
into the house, the lights came on in
the kitchen. It was Mommy. Grandpa
quickly hid behind some bushes.

He waited and waited. The kitchen
lights seemed to stay on forever. It
was cold! Suddenly, he noticed a
ladder leaning against the house. He
carefully and quietly moved the ladder
over toward the guestroom window.

Grandpa then tucked the bags of candy carefully inside his shirt, grabbed onto the ladder and started climbing up. He pulled himself onto the roof and reached out to open the window. But the window was locked. What would he do now? And then he saw the chimney. A clever idea popped into his head. He slowly crawled over, pulled himself up to the chimney top and then climbed in feet first. He was still holding on to the top of the chimney, but as soon as he lowered himself all the way into it, something bad happened. He got stuck. And one of the bags of candy broke open. The pieces began to drop one by one into the living room fireplace.

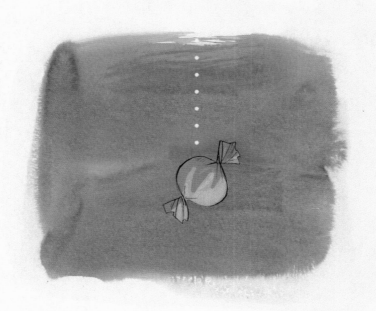

When the firemen arrived at the house they climbed a giant ladder up to the roof and pointed their bright flashlights into the chimney. It was quiet for a few seconds as they all looked at Grandpa squinting up at them. He was stuck halfway in the chimney.

"Who do you think you are," the chief asked, "Santa Claus?" Then it happened. One man giggled like a little girl...and then everyone started laughing. Oh, did they laugh.

A big burly fireman threw Grandpa a rope and told him to wrap it around himself under his arms. After a few minutes Grandpa was out and the fireman helped him climb down the ladder. Pieces of candy dropped out of his shirt with every step.

The firemen had Grandpa sit in their truck while they wrote up a report. He was sad and very embarrassed. He asked the firemen, "Is this Grandpa's timeout?" "Yes!" said the chief, with a twinkle in his eye.

The next morning Mommy sent Grandpa and the boys outside to play. She thought that was a safe idea. The boys were running around in the big yard when suddenly Grandpa noticed a nice big climbing tree. He said, "Let's climb that tree. I will show you how."

By now the boys had learned their lesson and told Grandpa that Mommy said they weren't allowed to climb that tree, and they were going to obey her. Grandpa said that was a good idea for them, but he still wanted to climb the tree. So he made his way up, branch by branch. It was a long climb and made the boys nervous because some of the branches cracked a little when Grandpa put his full weight on them. (He was a little chubby...)

Ohh

First his foot tripped, but he was able to grab a limb just before his big bottom landed on a limb. But both limbs broke with a loud CRACK—first the one he was kind of sitting on and then the one he was trying to hold. Grandpa howled like a hound dog as he banged into limbs all the way to the ground. Everything seemed to hurt all at once: his foot, his arm, his head...and his bottom. He was crying and in a lot of pain. David yelled for Johnny to run inside and get Mommy and Grandma.

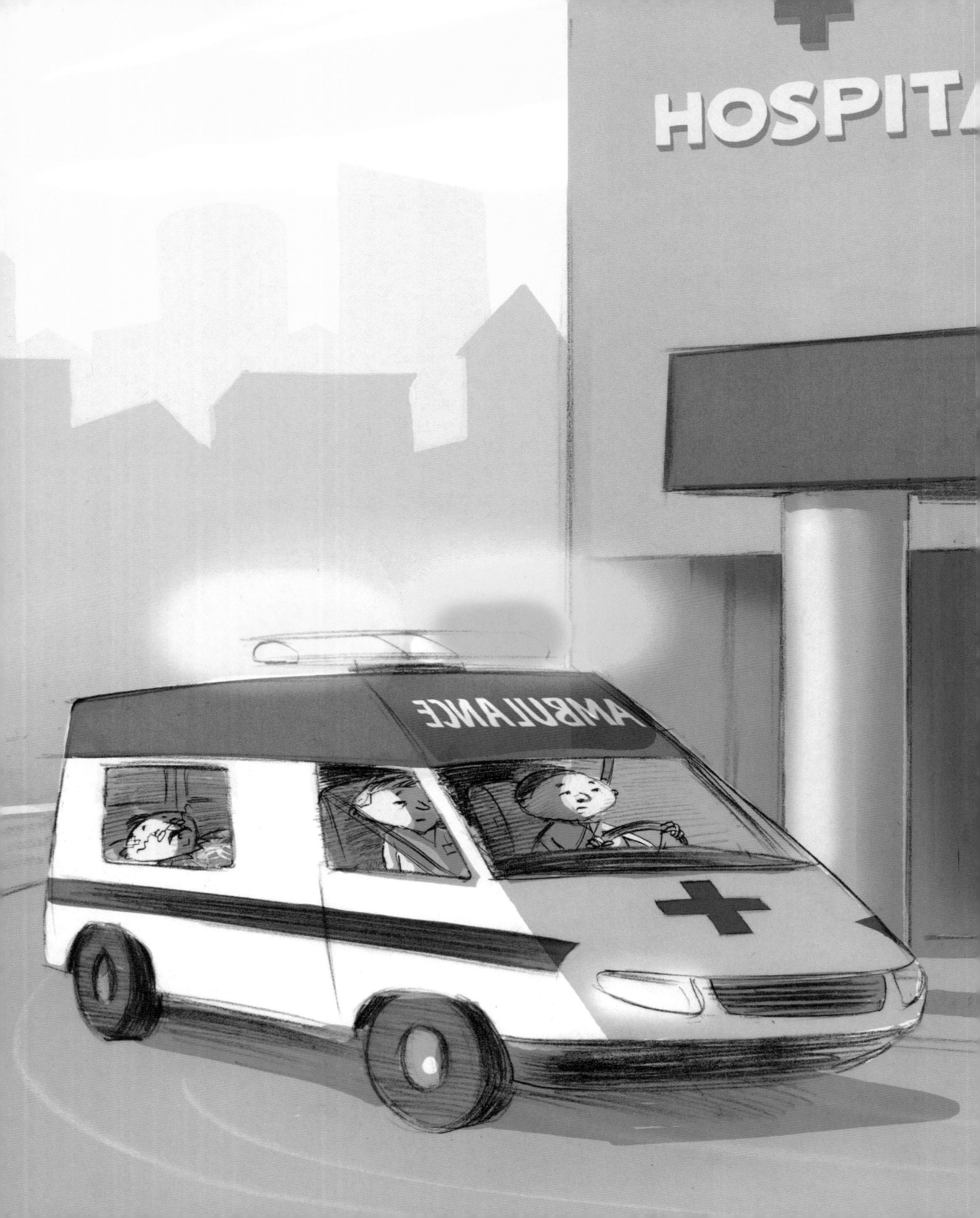
HOSPITA
AMBULANCE

EMERGENC

The ambulance arrived in minutes and took Grandpa to the hospital with all the lights blazing and siren blaring.

It didn't make him feel any better.

Later that evening, Mommy and the boys went to the hospital to visit Grandpa. He was lying in bed with a leg in a cast, an arm in a cast, a white bandage around his head and a giant soft pillow under his bottom. Grandma was nearby reading in a chair. His eyes were closed. The boys looked at him in shocked silence. Finally, Michael walked slowly up to the bed and nervously whispered, "Is this your worst timeout ever?"

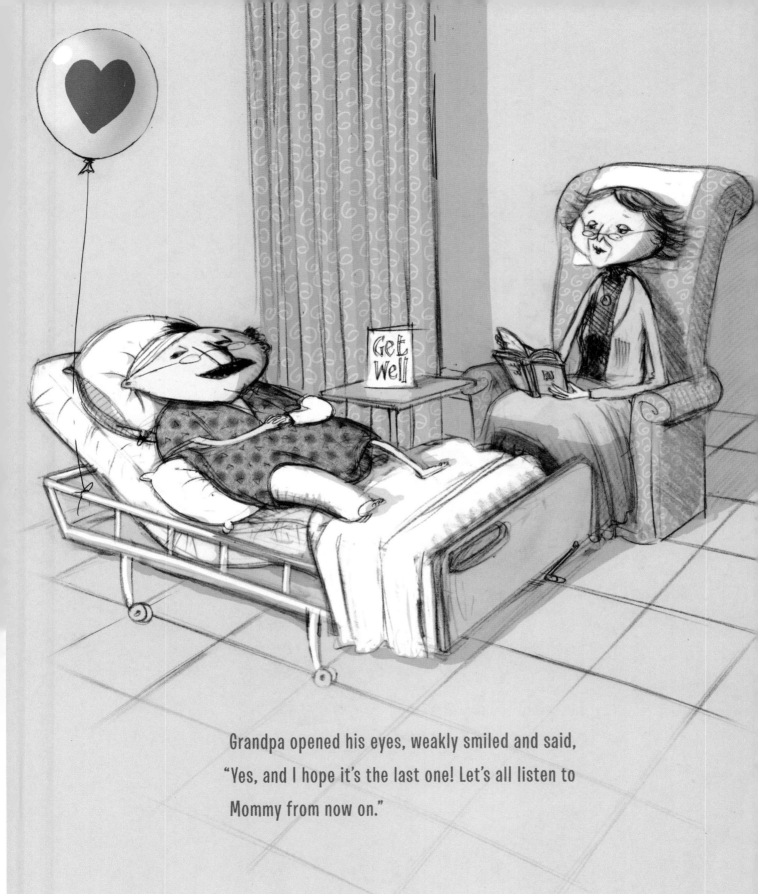

Grandpa opened his eyes, weakly smiled and said,
"Yes, and I hope it's the last one! Let's all listen to
Mommy from now on."

David and Johnny ran up to the bed and all the boys
held onto the arm without a cast. If Grandpa was
going to have a timeout, then they would all have
a timeout until he got better.

Follow
GRANDPA
on his many adventures...

GRANDPA THE BOOKWORM
And the World's Most Amazing Book

One windy day as Grandpa the Bookworm is playing in the backyard with his friends, he is suddenly lifted by a powerful gust and sent soaring into the air. When he finally comes down, he finds himself in the great house nearby where he lands on the pages of a huge book. Just when things are starting to look up, disaster strikes… **WHAM!** the book is suddenly closed, leaving Grandpa trapped inside.

How is Grandpa to ever make it back to his family and friends? Luckily, bookworms can make a second home in a book. But can he manage to survive on his own in such a big one? Learn how Grandpa finds help and encouragement on his journey through the world's most amazing book.

Captivating drawings by award-winning illustrator Tim Ladwig help bring this enchanting tale to life.

GRANDPA, HOW BIG IS YOUR LOVE?

Hunter loves exploring and asking questions. He's the kind of kid who always wants to know how everything works. One day his Grandpa tells him, "I love you." And, of course, Hunter immediately wants to know how much.

And so begins a quest for Grandpa to explain just how big his love for Hunter is.

Through many fanciful illustrations, Hunter learns how loud Grandpa's love is, how bright it shines, and how long it will last. But when they take a fall during a climb up a mountain, Hunter learns his most important lesson about how big Grandpa's love is.

GRANDPA SAVES THE DAY

When Grandpa and the family fly to Spain to watch the annual running of the bulls, they have no idea what is in store for them. The famous event begins as usual with crowds of people lining the streets shouting and waving scarves. Soon the sound of hooves can be heard coming closer and closer. Then as the bulls arrive, disaster strikes as they take an unexpected turn and head straight toward Grandpa and his grandkids!

With only seconds to act, Grandpa proves that he is willing to do whatever it takes to protect those he loves, even if it means putting himself in danger. Readers young and old will enjoy this humorous adventure about love and sacrifice.

OXVISION
BOOKS